Now You Know Science

Magnet Magic

Terry Jennings

W
FRANKLIN WATTS
LONDON•SYDNEY

This edition 2013

Franklin Watts
338 Euston Road, London NW1 3BH

Franklin Watts Australia
Level 17/207 Kent St, Sydney, NSW 2000

Copyright © Franklin Watts 2009

Created by Taglines Creative Ltd: Jean Coppendale and Honor Head
Written by: Terry Jennings
Design: Paul Manning

ISBN: 978 1 4451 2320 2

Dewey classification: 538'.4

A CIP catalogue for this book is available from the British Library.

Picture credits
t=top b=bottom l=left r=right

Cover: Franklin Watts;
3, 26, Scott Rothstein, Shutterstock; 5, 9l, Iofoto, Shutterstock; 7tl, AllPhoto, Shutterstock;
7tr, Mitzy, Shutterstock; 7bl, Ayazad, Shutterstock; 7br, Pablo Ede, Shutterstock;
8l, 28br, Thomas Mounsey, Shutterstock; 8r, 28bl, Ibne Handel, Shutterstock;
9tl, 28tl, Dole, Shutterstock; 9tr, Prism 68, Shutterstock; 9b, Pablo H. Caridad, Shutterstock;
10, Nicholas Piccillo, Shutterstock; 11, 12, 13, 14, 15, 19, Terry Jennings; 16l, Artproem, Shutterstock;
16r, Trailexplorers, Shutterstock; 17, Rob Marmion, Shutterstock; 18, Graca Victoria, Shutterstock;
20, Carlos Caetano, Shutterstock; 21, Fred Goldstein, Shutterstock; 22, Awe Inspiring Images,
Shutterstock; Franklin Watts; 24, Jeremy Walker/Science Photo Library; 25, Holger Mette,
Shutterstock; 27, Maxx-Studio, Shutterstock.

Printed in China

Franklin Watts is a division of Hachette Children's Books, an Hachette UK company.
www.hachette.co.uk

Contents

What is a magnet?

A magnet is a piece of iron or steel that can pull some materials towards it.

circular magnet

horseshoe magnet

button magnets

fridge magnets

▲ **Magnets come in all shapes and sizes.**

Magnets can pick up things. When something is picked up by a magnet, we say the magnet has attracted it.

bar magnet

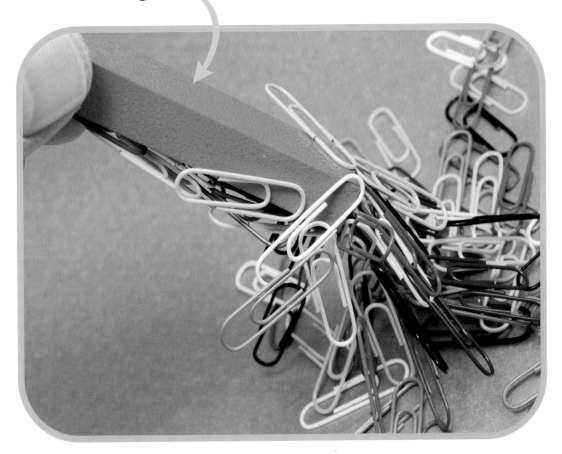

▲ **The bar magnet has attracted the paperclips.**

Magnetic and non-magnetic

Magnets will only attract objects made of steel and iron. These are called magnetic materials.

▼ **Steel and iron are both metals that are magnetic. Aluminium is also a metal but it is not magnetic.**

steel nails

aluminium can

Lots of materials are not attracted to a magnet. These are called non-magnetic materials.

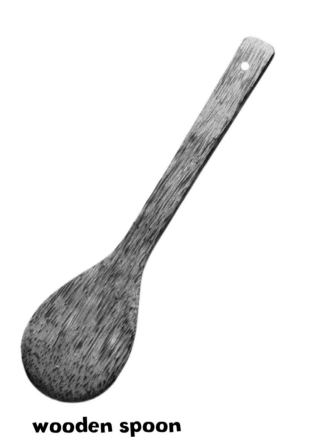

wooden spoon

paper bag

▲ These objects will not be attracted to a magnet.

plastic comb

Sorting materials

You can sort materials by whether they are magnetic or non-magnetic.

wood

plastic

steel

Which of these do you think would be attracted to a magnet?

Some keys are made of steel. Other keys are made of a metal called brass, which is non-magnetic.

▲ **You can use a magnet to sort materials. This magnet has attracted this key. Is the key made of brass or steel?**

Magnet poles

The two ends of a magnet are called its poles.
Every magnet has a north pole and a south pole.

north pole

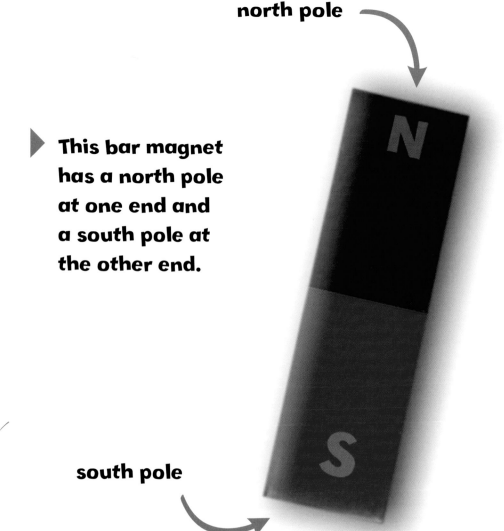

▶ **This bar magnet
has a north pole
at one end and
a south pole at
the other end.**

south pole

The south pole of one magnet will attract the north pole of another magnet.

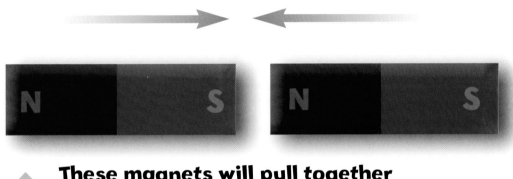

▲ These magnets will pull together or attract.

Two north poles or two south poles push each other away. We say they repel each other.

▲ These magnets will push apart or repel.

Magnetic forces

The push or pull of a magnet is called a magnetic force. Magnetic forces can pass through lots of different materials.

card

▲ **The force of this magnet can pass through the card and move the key.**

Magnetic forces can pass through non-magnetic materials such as wood, paper, plastic and glass.

plastic

▲ **This magnet is outside the plastic tumbler and is attracting the key inside the tumbler.**

Hidden magnets

There are lots of magnets where you cannot see them. Many things in the home use an electric motor to work. Every electric motor has a magnet in it.

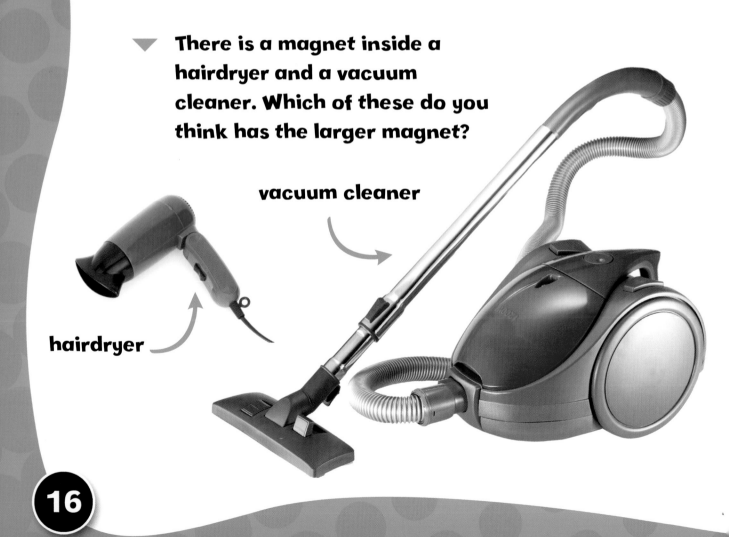

There is a magnet inside a hairdryer and a vacuum cleaner. Which of these do you think has the larger magnet?

vacuum cleaner

hairdryer

Magnets help a computer and a television set to work.

▲ **Magnets help this computer to store information.**

Useful magnets

Magnets can be used in many ways at home. Some tin-openers have magnets in them.

magnet

The top of the steel can is attracted to the magnet in the can-opener. This means that the top doesn't fall when the can is opened.

Some screwdrivers have a magnet on the end.

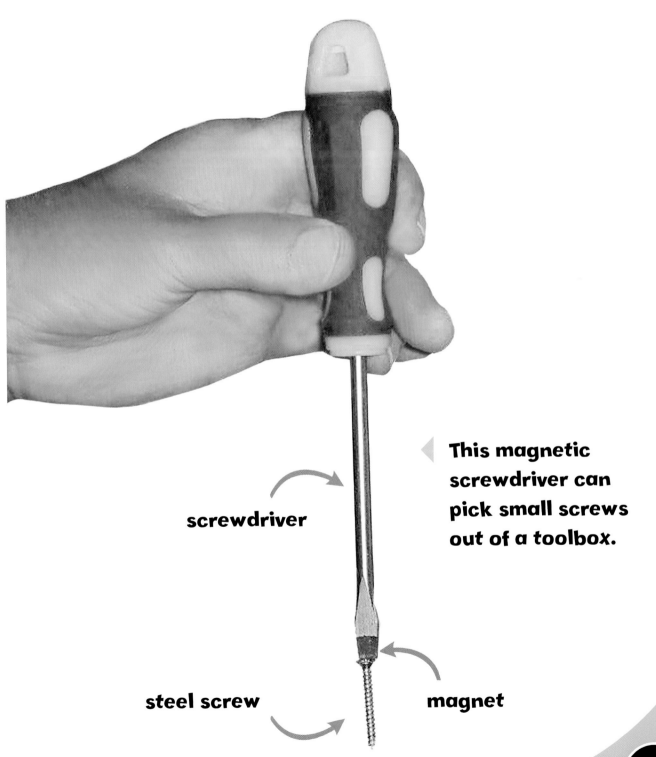

screwdriver

This magnetic screwdriver can pick small screws out of a toolbox.

steel screw

magnet

Fridge magnets

Magnets work on the door of a refrigerator because the door is made of thin steel.

fridge magnet

▲ **Fridge magnets can be used to keep notes and pictures on the fridge door.**

Hidden strip magnets also hold a refrigerator door shut.

strip magnets

▲ **Magnets keep the doors of these supermarket refrigerators closed so they stay cold inside.**

Weak and strong magnets

Magnets have different strengths. Some magnets are weak. This means they cannot pick up so many objects.

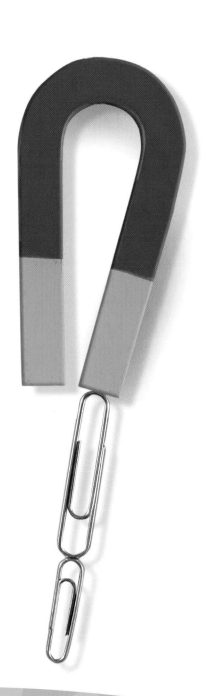

▶ **This horseshoe magnet has picked up just two paperclips.**

Some magnets are very strong and can pick up lots of objects.

▲ **This magnet is small but has picked up lots of paperclips. Size does not tell us how strong a magnet is.**

Electromagnets

Some magnets use electricity to switch them on. They are called electromagnets.

This huge electromagnet is being used in a scrap-metal yard. It is switched on to pick up and move large pieces of iron and steel.

magnet

iron and steel

Electromagnets are used to make some trains move along.

magnets are under here

▲ **This train uses electromagnets to move it forwards.**

Compasses

A compass has a needle that is a tiny magnet. The compass needle always points north. This is because there is iron at the centre of the Earth, which acts like a giant magnet.

▲ **You can use a compass to make sure you don't get lost.**

North, south, east and west are directions on a compass. They help us to find where we are going.

▼ **Which way is the blue compass needle pointing?**

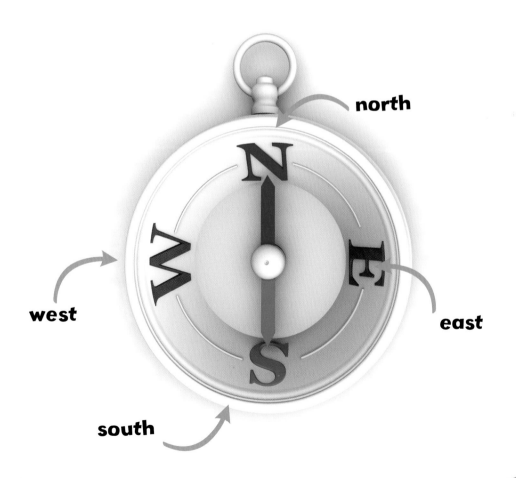

north

west

east

south

Things to do

Pick-ups

Which of these objects could you pick up with a magnet?

wooden spoon

a

steel key

b

aluminium can

c

plastic comb

d

Magnet match

Match the two ends of the magnet that will repel each other.

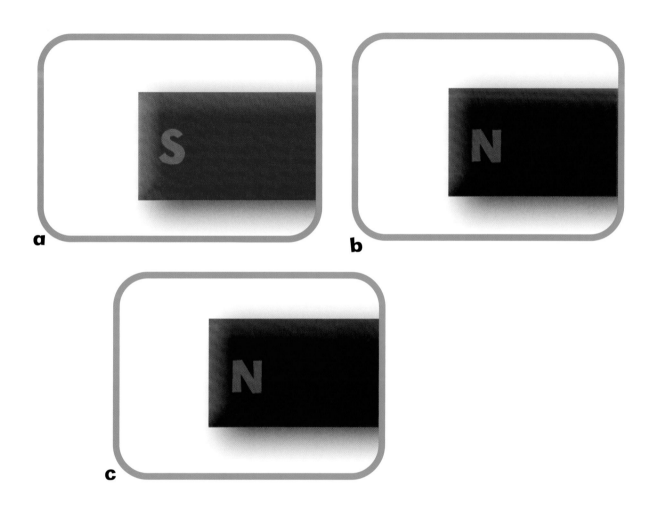

a
b
c

Talk back

Is this book magnetic or non-magnetic?

What are some good uses for a magnet?

Can you see any magnets now?

What are they used for?

Glossary

aluminium A silvery, non-magnetic metal.

compass An object containing a small magnet that helps you find the way.

iron A strong metal that is magnetic.

metals Materials that are hard and shiny.

scrap-metal yard A place where old metal is sorted and reused or recycled.

steel A magnetic metal that is made from iron.

Index